D0108293

THE WINE LOG

CHRISTOPHER PAVONE

The Lyons Press
Guilford, Connecticut
An imprint of The Globe Pequot Press

The Lyons Press is an imprint of The Globe Pequot Press.

Printed in the United States of America

10 9 8 7 6 5 4 3

**Library of Congress
Cataloging-in-Publication Data**

Pavone, Christopher.
    The wine log / Christopher Pavone.
        p. cm.
    Includes index.
    ISBN 1-55821-686-3
    1. Wine and winemaking. I. Title.
TP548.P32 1999
641.2'2—dc21   98-31309
                                                  CIP

Contents

Introduction

*I*t's a special occasion, so we've chosen an elegant and not inexpensive restaurant. Menus are handed around, to the ladies first, of course, and then someone—damn his soul—says, "Chris, why don't you choose the wine?" The sommelier presents me with a daunting leatherbound volume, and I begin turning the pages, slowly at first but with increasing haste, anxiously searching for a familiar name, although I know at heart that there will be none. I begin to perspire—no, that is too delicate a word: I begin to sweat.

Before I know it, the waiter has been dismissed twice because I haven't even *glanced* at the food menu. I've come to the end of the list and still have no idea what the hell we're going to drink—for the *first* bottle: I'm pretty sure I'll need to make at least *two* choices, unless my first is so abominable that I will suffer the indignity of having my privileges revoked.

Panic sweeps over me, and I randomly turn to the middle of the book—Australian (?) and New

Zealand (!) reds. Not a chance; I didn't even know they *made* wine. Another page—ah, California, sunny California, home of . . . a bewildering variety of wines. Everyone is growing unsympathetically impatient, and I don't have the luxury to do more than glance at the names and the vintages. I scan the price column and shudder at some of the figures. I briefly consider closing my eyes and letting my finger land where it may, but I'm afraid someone will notice this not-very-sophisticated decision-making stratagem. In grave despair—my night ruined, without question—I make a choice based on a ridiculous but, I hope, pardonable criterion: the second least expensive—not the *cheapest*, for the love of God—wine on the page.

I lay down the book, announce my selection—raised eyebrow, "Very good, monsieur" with more than a hint of sarcasm. Already, I can't remember what I've chosen. When the bottle is presented, I smile at the label, sniff the cork ignorantly, nodding like an imbecile, and swig the little half-ounce. I try to collect my poise, but far too flummoxed to speak, I merely nod even more effusively.

I have no idea what I'm doing.

No one is born a wine connoisseur—complete with finely tuned taste buds, a memory expertly trained to dissect, absorb, and imprint wines' attributes, an encyclopedic knowledge of the history and geography of wine making, a thorough understanding of the minute details and variations of the agriculture and production, and the many other subcategories of expertise that constitute a complete education. Most people, at one point or another and possibly many times, have confronted a restaurant's wine list, or the even more overwhelming selections in a wine shop, with *absolutely no idea* how to make a choice.

This is a frustrating state of affairs. But as with beginning an exercise regimen, or starting a new career, there is very little to be gained by standing on the precipice, anxiously contemplating the fall. Take a first step.

That first step, for increasing an appreciation and understanding of wine, is the simple act of *remembering* what you drink. This doesn't mean studying the technical aspects of viticulture or enology, nor memorizing the châteaux of Bordeaux or Burgundy, nor poring over the columns and reviews that appear everywhere from daily newspapers to specialized magazines. To get started, it is important that you establish some basic standards by which you appreciate and judge wine. These standards should always be your own personal ones, based on your own tasting and, well, your own taste. And the initial process of developing these standards is nothing more than remembering the tastes of wines from one bottle to the next.

Accurately remembering wine requires that you taste it with heightened awareness, focusing attention on the way it looks, smells, tastes, and feels. It's also helpful, although a bit more involved, to attempt to isolate the different elements within each sensation—for instance, that the taste includes elements of tobacco, oak, and blackberry. Recognizing these subtle characteristics is a skill that, like any other, you will develop with practice and patience. But such a skill is much more than a mnemonic aid: it is also a part of what makes drinking wine an enjoyable experience.

Perhaps just as important is the process of translating these sensory experiences into language—formulating, at least in your mind, words to describe the sensations. Taking the next step and writing down those words not only reinforces your memory, but also provides you with a record of them.

By paying attention to the sensory experiences and translating them into language, you will undoubtedly increase the enjoyment of individual wines. But in order to build these single-tasting memories into a full understanding of wine, it is important to retain not only the subjective sensations but also the objective attributes (winery, vintage, predominant grape, and so forth). For instance, you must remember not only that you found Friday night's wine watery looking, a bit medicinal smelling, and tasting unpleasantly of moss, but also who made the wine, when, where, and, usually, from what grapes.

With just the sensory memories, you may form a very broad base of opinions about how wine tastes, smells, and whatnot, and what you like and dislike.

But you won't be able to find or recognize these characteristics, on the label, without tasting. And, unfortunately, we must usually choose wines before tasting them.

To further complicate matters, we (at least *I*) don't usually drink wine in a vacuum, but rather amid other influential factors, such as the restaurant's list and suggestion, the choice made by friends in their home, the food, the atmosphere in which it is consumed, and, of course, the price.

So now you've paid attention to all these things: you've admired the wine's color and hue; you've inhaled deeply and detected its aroma; you've taken a sip, gurgled, swallowed, and analyzed its component flavors; you've attended to how it feels; you've read and reread its label and memorized the winery, region, country, vintage, varietal; you've noted the atmosphere, the food, the cost . . . And you've probably collected far more information than you can absorb without some assistance.

This book will provide you with that assistance: a way to record this information and use it later. On the pages that follow, write down all the above—the objective, defining particulars of the wine, your subjective impressions of it, and any other factors that influence your memory and enjoyment of a wine—in whatever vocabulary comes to mind easily and will be recognizable in the future.

Wine connoisseurs and professionals have developed a vocabulary of tasting adjectives (to say nothing of the specialized nouns of geography, manufacturers, and viticulture) that may seem far-fetched and intimidating. But this language, like all argots, serves a utilitarian purpose: these agreed-upon terms enable discussion about perceptual nuances that can be universally understood. Eskimos, famously, developed an astounding vocabulary on the subject of snow, because being able to discuss snow is important; so, too, do enologists require a specialized vocabulary to discuss wine.

It is impossible to learn the usage of these terms from text alone; the only way is to taste a wine while reading or hearing its description in this vocabulary. But for the purposes of keeping your own personal wine log, the most important characteristics of your vocabulary are that it be *meaningful* and *consistent*— that the words come naturally, that you understand what you mean by them, and that later you will be able to associate a sensation with each word.

There is a glossary in the back of this book, which doesn't include tasting terms, but rather the more objective—*factual*, if you will—characteristics of the wine. Use the glossary as a guide to recognize the elements of a label, to *define* the incontestable specifics of a wine; but use your own vocabulary to describe the wine's sensations.

There is a long-standing debate over the use and merits of background knowledge as a means of appreciating art. One side argues that a work should speak for itself, that the viewer's appreciation should be based on nothing other than his own perceptions. The other side argues that it is impossible to fully appreciate a work without an in-depth understanding of its context. As may be the case with all such arguments, the truth probably lies somewhere in between.

With the consumption of wine, a great part of the matter lies in the simple impression from an uninformed swill. But another great part, no doubt, lies in the recognition of familiar characteristics, in the comparison to previously encountered subjects, in the informed knowledge of the history, geography, agriculture, and technology—in contexts both universal and personal.

The aim of this book is to help you develop these contexts, which in turn will greatly increase your appreciation of wine.

How to Use This Book

ORGANIZATION

*T*he note-taking pages are divided into parts for red, white, and sparkling wines. Technically, what we normally refer to as red and white wines are in the same overall category—they are *still wines*, with neither alcoholic fortification nor the effervescence of sparkling wines—but their attributes are quite distinct from each other, and it is helpful to keep track of them separately. The other category of wine, *fortified* (whose alcohol levels have been augmented), includes *port*, *sherry*, *brandy*, and *cognac*, among others. There is no section here for fortified wines, because they are sufficiently different from still or sparkling wines and are consumed in a markedly different manner, and therefore represent a different type of beverage—even though they are, in fact, wines.

Each note-taking page is organized into three sections, with (1) the most general, objective data at the top of the page; (2) the tasting section in the middle; and (3) the ancillary or background circumstances at the bottom.

(1) NOTE TAKING: THE LABEL, OR OBJECTIVE ATTRIBUTES

The only piece of objective data that is open to interpretation is price, which can vary from establishment to establishment, and differs wildly from a restaurant to a wine shop. Expect at least a 100 percent markup from shops to restaurants, and the more extensive the restaurant's list—the more inventory in which the restaurant invests that will not produce short-term income—the greater the markup. For the purposes of comparing wines' prices, it will be helpful to distinguish between restaurant and shop prices— perhaps with *R* or *S* following the dollar figure—and even to comment (at *Where*) on establishments' general prices and extensiveness of wine selection.

The name, vintner, vintage, country, and region are not open to interpretation—but they are *wide* open to misreading. On the following pages are some typical labels with annotations pointing out their components. The types of information that labels contain differ vastly, not only by country but by region and other factors. To become truly comfortable with labels, it is important to develop a rudimentary vocab-

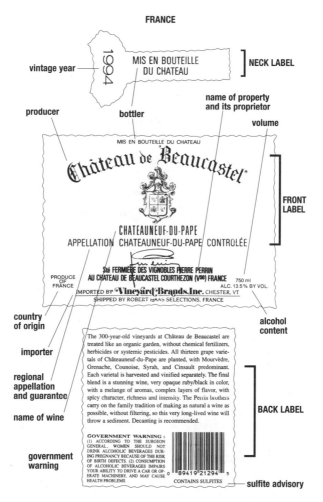

FRANCE

producer   name of wine   vintage year   regional appellation and guarantee

CHATEAU FONROQUE

GRAND CRU CLASSÉ

SAINT-ÉMILION GRAND CRU
APPELLATION SAINT-ÉMILION GRAND CRU CONTROLÉE

1995

G.F.A. CHATEAU FONROQUE, PROPRIÉTAIRE A St-EMILION - GIRONDE - FRANCE

J.A CURAT et J.J. MOUEIX - Gérants

MIS EN BOUTEILLES A LA PROPRIÉTÉ

LF 95085

RED BORDEAUX WINE   750 ML   ALC. 13.5% BY VOL.
IMPORTED BY : WILLIAM GRANT & SONS INC. NEW YORK, N.Y.
SHIPPED BY : ETS JEAN-PIERRE MOUEIX, LIBOURNE FRANCE
PRODUCE OF FRANCE   CONTAINS SULFITES

volume

type of wine   alcohol content
    bottler   sulfite advisory

importer   country of origin   name of property and its proprietors

ITALY

name of wine

vintage year

bottler

regional appellation and guarantee

1993

VIGNETO ARBORINA DELL'ANNUNZIATA

BAROLO

DENOMINAZIONE D'ORIGINE CONTROLLATA E GARANTITA

IMBOTTIGLIATO ALL'ORIGINE
DAL PRODUTTORE E VITICULTORE

GIANFRANCO BOVIO

ANNUNZIATA - LA MORRA (ITALIA)
ITALIA

NET CONTENT 750 ML ℮ - ITALIA - CONTAINS SULFITES
PRODUCT OF ITALY - RED WINE - ALCOHOL 13,5% BY VOLUME

sulfite advisory

volume

type of wine

alcohol content

producer (and location)

country of origin

ulary of wine terms, including the major regions in the important wine-producing countries, the most popular grape varieties, and a few foreign words that will assist in identifying the components of a label. The most essential of these terms appear in the glossary.

Producer

Usually the best way to identify a wine is by the full name—first and last—of the producer: a winery, or estate (*château* or *domaine* in French; *fattoria* or *masseira* in Italian; *Weingut* in German; *bodega* in Spanish). The winery may produce a number of different wines, in which case those wine names will be quite prominent.

Name

The individual product can be one of the most elusive pieces of information on the label. In North and South America, Australia, New Zealand, some other New World areas, and a few distinct regions in Europe, a wine is often named for its *varietal*, or dominant grape—*merlot*, *cabernet sauvignon*, or *chardonnay*, for example. This practice is almost always subject to regional laws that dictate a minimum ratio, usually 75 percent, of that varietal; wines that don't meet the specified threshold can't use the name of the grape (this is *not* an indicator of quality). In these cases, the wine is often given an abstract or generic name—such as *reserve*, *late harvest*, or *table wine*—or is *vineyard-*

designated (named for the vineyard); this too requires that a certain ratio, usually 95 percent, of the grapes come from the designated vineyard.

In most of Europe, wines are usually named for their designated growing areas—such as *Bordeaux, Chianti,* or *Rioja*—which are defined by law and whose wine production is overseen by governing bodies with strict standards. In France, the organization is *Appellation d'Origine Contrôlée* (AOC or AC); in Italy, *Denominazione di Origine Controllata* (DOC) or *Denominazione di Origine Controllata e Garantita* (DOCG); in Spain, *Denominación de Origen* (DO) or *Denominación de Origen Calificada* (DOCa); and in Portugal, *Denominaçao de Origem Controlada* (DOC). In the United States, the *American Viticultural Area* (AVA) might be considered an equivalent, but American wines are rarely named for AVAs (although the designation may appear as supplementary description on the label), and the AVAs impose almost no standards on production.

Along with the specific name of the wine, the label may indicate an even broader designation of the *type* of wine—*red Bordeaux wine*, for example.

Vintage

The vintage of a wine indicates the year in which the grapes were harvested, which usually is also the year in which the wine was made. A certain ratio (usually 95 percent) of the grapes used in a vintage-designated wine must be harvested from that single year, or the wine is designated *N.V.*—nonvintage. Many Champagnes and other sparkling wines are nonvintage—made from blends, or *cuvées*, that include grapes or mixed wines from different years. In such circumstances, the absence of vintage shouldn't be taken as a reflection of a wine's quality; but when a vintage *is* given, it is most definitely a defining aspect of the wine.

Country and Region

This will usually be clear immediately, from the language. Wines sold in the United States are required by law to specify the country of origin on the label. The region within the country isn't legally required, but is nevertheless usually noted. As mentioned previously, the name of many European wines *is* its region. With wines that are named for varietals or are given other nonregional names, the region often appears prominently—*Napa Valley*, *Finger Lakes*, or *Hunter Valley*, for example.

Other Information

The labels on the preceding pages identify some items for which there are no entries on the tasting pages in this book. It's important to be able to understand what these items are, but it's rarely important to keep track of them.

Alcohol Content: For table wines, the legal range in the United States is 7 to 14 percent; for fortified wines, the range is 17 to 20 percent. The relative alcoholic strength of the wine will be apparent by taste, and is indeed one of the defining factors to note while tasting. It is not, however, often helpful to keep track of the exact percentage.

Volume: May appear on the bottle's glass rather than on the label. The *standard wine bottle* is 750 milliliters, or 25.4 ounces, which is similar in size to the *fifth* (four-fifths of a quart) that is often used for distilled spirits. Other common sizes are the *half-bottle* (375 milliliters) and the *magnum* (1.5 liters, or two standard bottles). Others range from a *split*, which is one-quarter of a standard bottle, to a *Nebuchadnezzar*, which at 15 liters is equal to twenty standard bottles. Noting the volume is often useful with nonstandard bottles, to be able to compare prices.

Importer and Shipper: Only indicated for wines not produced in the United States, and worth noting if you happen to fall in love with a particular wine and despair of its availability.

Bottler: Usually the same as the producer, in which case the label states *estate bottled* (*mis en bouteille au domaine* or *mis en bouteille du château* in French; *imbottigliato all'origine* in Italian; and *Gutsabfüllung* or *Erzeugerabfüllung* in German). Such wines are usually of a superior quality to those whose grapes have been grown and wine made by one entity and bottled by another. But in certain growing areas— Alsace, for example—there are many high-quality winemakers that are too small to bottle wines individually, and such vintners use the services of a bottler. Without knowing a given region's particular state of affairs, whether or not a wine is estate bottled isn't a reliable indicator of quality.

Sulfite Advisory: If a wine contains more than a minimum amount of sulfites, to which some people may have severe allergic reactions, it is legally required in the United States for the label to state so. Sulfites are salts of sulfurous acid, which is used in viticulture and wine production.

Government Warning: This notice regarding the various hazards associated with alcoholic beverages is also required by law in the United States.

Even More Information

Sometimes the label will indicate a generic type of wine—*table wine* or *dry white wine*, for example— that is only of interest if you're having trouble identifying the general category; such descriptions should never be interpreted as a mark of quality or lack of it. The same can be said about other descriptive phrases that may appear on the label—ranging from simple statements such as *special reserve* to much more ornate claims about the process by which the wine was produced or its quality.

(2) NOTE TAKING: TASTING

Wine tasting is actually a combination of four senses, only one of which is what we normally call taste. (And with sparkling wines, you can even give a try to the fifth sense—hearing.)

Sight

Use a plain, unadorned wineglass—not colored, etched, or otherwise decorated crystal, which may be attractive but will inhibit clear viewing. Most wineglasses curl inward at the top, which helps capture the aromas and also prevents the liquid from spilling out while you're swirling. Fill the glass with a couple of ounces, and no more than a third full; leaving empty space not only allows room for swirling, but also allows your nose access to the bowl.

Tilt the glass at a forty-five-degree angle, viewing against a white background (a tablecloth or napkin). Look at the line at which the liquid ends, called the *rim*, where the color will be most apparent. The *depth*, or strength, of the color is usually a very good indicator of the wine's richness. Then study the *hue*, which is usually a good indicator of the wine's maturity, or age: young red wine will often be nearly purple, but will lose this vivid coloring with age and turn to crimson and deep red, and when fully mature to brick and reddish brown; white wines, on the other hand, darken with age, from greenish yellow through straw to gold and eventually amber or brown.

Then judge the *clarity*, or degree of *brilliance*: the wine should be free of cloudiness or suspended particles, and should sparkle when struck by light. This is often described on a continuum from *cloudy* to *limpid* and *brilliant*. (But note that long-aged wines, particularly reds, will develop sediment, which you can filter by *decanting:* allow the bottle to rest upright for an hour or so, then slowly pour the contents into another container, leaving the final few ounces—with the sediment—behind in the original bottle.)

Now swirl the wine. The easiest way to do this is to place the foot of the glass on the table with your palm firmly resting across the top of the foot and your fingers splayed on either side of the stem. Move your hand in a small circle (no more than a half-inch in diameter), applying slight pressure with your palm to keep the glass on the table and the liquid from spilling.

After a few seconds, stop swirling and notice the wine's *legs*, or the trail that the wine leaves in the glass. Young, thin wines will leave nary a trace in the wake of swirling; more mature wines will leave slowly dissipating waves, sometimes appearing almost viscous, called *sheets*. Legs usually indicate richness and full body.

Smell

This swirling has also served the more important purpose of freeing up the molecules, mixing them with oxygen, and thus releasing the wine's aroma, preparing the wine for what may be—perhaps oxymoronically—the most important aspect of wine "tasting."

The human sense of smell has a much wider capacity to analyze components and ranges of intensity than does our taste. Experienced wine tasters harness this power and train their noses to isolate different levels of many distinct scents. They also develop a language link to associate those scents with words. (There is even a product available—though not widely, and not inexpensively—that contains samples of many different aromas found in wine, for nose-training purposes.)

A nose trained for sniffing wine is a valuable resource that takes time to develop. The payoff, however, is great: it drastically increases the ability to analyze, remember, and enjoy wine. It will also enhance other aspects of life—most notably eating and spending time in the outdoors—and should not be thought of as simply a "wine sense."

Now smell the glass of wine. (Do not smell wine from the bottle, at least not immediately after opening: the air in there may have been stagnating for a long time, with some chemical processes going on to boot, and will probably not exude an appealing aroma; this is normal, and will dissipate over a few minutes. If the wine is *corked*—turned rancid—the unpleasant aroma will not dissipate.) It's best to dip your nose slightly into the bowl of the glass for just a quick preliminary whiff; beginning with a long breath can be overwhelming.

Lean back and think about what you've just smelled. Don't judge merely whether or not you found it pleasant, but also try to separate the components. The main categories are fruits, herbs and spices, woods, and flowers. The wine is not actually composed of these elements, mind you, but it does contain the same flavor compounds. It is just as proper (or improper) to say that a piece of chocolate—made from only cocoa beans and milk—has elements of the cabernet sauvignon as it is to say vice versa; the chocolate does not contain wine and the wine does not contain chocolate, but they both share the same or similar compounds.

Now bring your nose back to the glass and take a full, deep, leisurely snort. Again, move away from the glass and take some time to contemplate the various elements. A few dominant aromas will probably present themselves, usually of fruit and wood. You may catch hints of different varieties of each, along with lesser components. Sniff again, confirm your impressions, and take note of them.

The language for this phase of tasting can be straightforward—the vocabulary is of everyday, naturally occurring substances. But determining the exact scents—and the words for them—can also be quite elusive: since most of us are not accustomed to relying on our sense of smell to identify things, we may not be able to readily locate a memory of a parallel scent. This is especially problematic for city dwellers, who probably don't often encounter many of the natural substances. Practice, however, will bring adeptness.

Taste

Finally, the moment we've all been waiting for: actually inserting the wine into the mouth. Take a large enough sip to be able to fully taste the liquid,

but not so large that you won't have room to com-
fortably swirl it around in your mouth by moving
your tongue. Do not swallow.

We have taste buds throughout our mouths,
but we detect different categories of tastes—sweet,
sour, bitter, and salty—in specific regions.

Sweetness, the extent of *residual sugars*, is detected
at the tip of the tongue, and so is one of the first tastes
we encounter. Its degree is most commonly referred
to on the continuum of *bone dry* to *overly sweet*,
with the word *dry* indicating the relative absence of
noticeable sugars. Sweetness is more important in
white wines than in reds, which often have very little
or no residual sugars.

Sourness, the degree of *acidity*, is apparent on
the sides of the tongue and at the back of the throat, as
well as in the cheek area, and so will not be fully tasted
without either swallowing or swirling the wine around
in the mouth. A certain degree of acidity is desirable,
providing complexity and, in whites, complementing
any sweetness. Too little acid in a wine, marked by
a noticeable excess of another element, is referred
to from *fat* and *plump* to *flabby;* the right amount of
acid contributes to a wine being *mellow* or *balanced*,
or if apparent but pleasant (usually for whites) *lively*
or *crisp;* and an excess of acid is referred to from
aggressive and *tart* to *sharp* and *acidic*—the same as
the unpleasant, acerbic taste of vinegar.

Bitterness, the effect of a wine's *tannins* (see
below), is detected in the middle of the tongue, but

in excess it can permeate the entire mouth. Too much will be noticeable, and undesirable, if it completely dominates the aftertaste.

Saltiness, the final of the four main categories of taste, shouldn't be present at all in wine.

Flavors that incorporate different combinations of these main categories will make themselves apparent at areas where the different taste buds merge. Fruit tastes, for instance, which are combinations of sweet and sour, can usually be noticed in the middle of the tongue—between the tip (sweet) and the sides and back (sour). So it is important to move the wine around in your mouth, being sure to cover all areas.

As you taste the wine, you will also notice the level of alcohol. Not enough of it will make other elements, particularly fruitiness, seem overpowering; if alcohol is low but this doesn't produce any negative effects, the wine is referred to as *light*. As the sensation of alcohol becomes too strong, it is referred to as *heady*, *brawny*, *heavy*, and finally *hot*, an unpleasant burning sensation.

Touch

Tannins are naturally occurring compounds in wine that are produced from the skins, pits, and stems— the solids—of the grapes, and also from the wood in which wines may be aged. Tannins are most prominent in reds, and they may not be present at all in some whites. The production of white wines entails removing the mashed grape juice, or *must*, from these solids very soon after pressing, and hence tannins are not very developed. (This is also the reason why the wine is white: grape juice is essentially colorless, and the color is produced when the juice ferments with the skin. Red- or black-skinned grapes can thus produce white wine.)

Tannins do much of the work in providing a wine with *structure*, or its ability to successfully incorporate many different elements into a unified taste, as well contribute to aging. (Which is why red wines, with tannins, often benefit from aging, while whites, without much in the way of tannins, often do not.)

Additionally, tannins possess the strange quality of being *felt* in the mouth more than *tasted:* they produce a slightly puckery, dry sensation in the middle-top part of the tongue, and perhaps all the way back to the throat. A certain level of tannins will be pleasing, and will provide a vehicle for the other tastes. But some wines, particularly young reds, can be overly tannic, producing a displeasing astringency throughout the mouth. Others, mainly whites and light, fruity reds, are noticeably free of tannins, and their general taste will usually seem imbalanced and incomplete. Noting the level of tannins should be an important part of tasting notes, running from *soft* through *firm* to *austere, hard, harsh,* and eventually downright *astringent.*

The overall texture of a wine—or the feeling of weight in the mouth—is referred to as *body*, and is perhaps the single most defining tasting characteristic of a wine. The degrees of tannins, acid, alcohol, and other elements all contribute to a wine's body, from *light-bodied* or *thin* to *rich, complex, well-rounded*, and *full-bodied*. This is the area of wine-tasting vocabulary that gets most creative. You might find words such as *insipid* and *masculine* being bandied about, although their meanings are often difficult to decipher. You don't have to use such terms for your own tasting notes: since the judgment of body is a very general impression, the description of body can be a very personal vocabulary choice.

Tannins also contribute to a wine's ability to maintain taste for a very long time after swallowing or spitting out—sometimes as much as a few minutes. The final strong taste is the wine's *finish;* the prolonged extension of the taste after the wine has vacated the mouth is the *aftertaste*, usually referred to as a degree of length or persistence, from *short* to *long*. If a wine is overly tannic, this will dominate the aftertaste.

Overall Impression

All of the above tasting criteria are, to lesser and greater extents, subjective; and none is more so than this final, most general opinion.

(3) NOTE TAKING: ATMOSPHERE

The *Date, Where,* and *Shared With* entries are not aspects of the wine itself, but they could help jog your memory. They also might end up being a valuable—albeit terse—record of social occasions.

Wine with Food

The *Served With* information can be quite important. Wine is best consumed with food; when well matched, one can—and *should*—greatly enhance the enjoyment of the other. The most sublime, full-bodied, mature cabernet sauvignon becomes all the more pleasing when paired with that tender but assertive and perfectly cooked rack of lamb. And that light, crisp, and flavorful sauvignon blanc is greatly enhanced with a delicately prepared, fork-tender fillet of sole.

Nonetheless, while there are general qualities that make certain wines and foods complementary, the choice is a personal one. Just as some people—including (if not *especially*) professional chefs—are attracted to what others might consider completely unlikely pairings of different food tastes and textures, so too do people have markedly different opinions on what is desirable in pairings of foods and wines. These are important considerations to develop, and you should diligently note your preferences.

When attending to these combinations, it is essential to pay particular attention to sauces, which may play a role far more important than the main ingredient in determining an apporpriate wine. This is an especially significant consideration when the main ingredient is a somewhat neutral vehicle for the sauce. Pasta, for example, may be lightly sauced with nutty olive oil, tender sweet pea shoots, and a dollop of milky ricotta, and this might be paired nicely with a woody white. Conversely, the same noodle tossed with a spicy *arrabiata* sauce heavy with acidic tomato, salty pancetta, and red-hot chili peppers would completely overwhelm any but the most sturdy red. A chicken grilled with acidic lemon and herbal thyme demands a thoroughly different wine than a *coq-au-vin* simmered in a tannic young red; tuna with briny capers and olives is vastly different from tuna broiled with a sweet balsamic glaze; veal can be delicate as cutlets in a mild delicate marsala or hearty and assertive as shanks in an earthy *osso buco*.

Some restaurant menus presume that you possess a certain degree of familiarity with traditional preparations, and thus don't provide explicit descriptions for, say, a chicken paillard or veal Milanese. If you find yourself unfamiliar with a given dish, consult the waitstaff for a description before choosing a wine. One way is to ask, for example, "How is the veal prepared?" Another alternative is to simply ask for a wine suggestion—and expect a reasoning behind the suggestion; if a waiter can't explain why a particular wine is nicely paired with a dish, the suggestion is probably based on some factor—price, markup, inventory, popularity— other than the best interests of your meal.

On the other hand, many restaurants offer in-depth descriptions of dishes. Occasionally, some of this may seem silly or irrelevant, but it is almost always of great value in determining a suitable wine pairing, and should be read carefully.

Perhaps the most significant impediment to choosing a complementary wine is the habit of most diners to order different dishes—often purposefully, and often wildly different. A foursome may be having sole almondine with a saffron pilaf, cherry-glazed duck breast with spicy chestnut stuffing, garlic-crusted rack of lamb with herbed mashed potatoes, and a citrus roast chicken with bitter greens. There is absolutely no chance that *any* wine is going to be complementary to each of these four entrées, and it is hopeless to try. In this type of situation, the more sensible approaches—barring ordering four individual bottles or half-bottles—are: ordering two different wines, thereby halving the number of dishes a wine must complement (in this case, the lamb and duck might share one wine, and the sole and chicken another); ordering a single nonassertive wine that will not greatly enhance any dish but will also not greatly overpower or be overpowered by any (and be sure not to spend much money on this); or ordering a wine that will complement the dish for the person who cares the most (and, of course, informing the others that this is going on).

WINE TASTING: FINAL WORDS

You should be aware of certain dangers that accompany developing a discerning wine palate. They include but are not limited to: habitually swirling many non-wine liquids, from morning's orange juice and coffee to evening's cocktail and *digestif*, and you should be careful not to hurt yourself (coffee and tea), ruin furniture, rugs, and clothing (a full glass of nearly anything), or embarrass yourself (absolutely anything, if *anybody* notices); using the price of a favorite wine as a yardstick by which to measure other expenditures (is the beach weekend worth that excellent-vintage case?); and analyzing the flavor components of almost anything (hmm . . . nice hint of oak in these Cheez Doodles).

But the most significant danger is becoming a "wine snob," a disease that can take many forms ranging from simply avoiding lesser wines and restaurants with mediocre lists to belittling people who don't know the difference and alienating friends in the process. It is certainly a pleasure to share a superb wine with like-minded aficionados, and may be a bit disappointing to "waste" a fine specimen on utter amateurs. Without exercising some restraint and tact, though, wine lovers may sooner or later find their social acquaintances limited to aficionados, and excluded of amateurs, and their worlds limited thusly.

Red Wines

To some, the ideal wine is a complex, full-bodied, fully aged Bordeaux from a *premier cru* estate—a 1945 Château Latour, for example. But a bottle of this will fetch at least two thousand dollars. Luckily, there are many superb wines from the world over that are in a more reasonable price range. Many of the most respected wines may be had for under a hundred dollars per bottle, and nearly every category of wine has excellent offerings under fifty, with some even in the twenty-dollar range. (Expect to pay at least twice the retail price in a restaurant.)

A wine's vintage is, of course, an important determination of its overall quality. But a wine's *age* is often presumed to be just as or even more important than other characteristics, as in "the older the better." This is not usually so: the vast majority—probably in the neighborhood of 95 percent—of wines produced today are meant to be and should be consumed within two years of production. Of the remaining tiny proportion, a vast majority are meant to be consumed within five years. In the end, it is probably fewer than one in a hundred wines that will benefit much from aging of more than five years—few and far in between.

The cost, the vintage, the age . . . such objective attributes may often do more in the way of dictating to people what they should enjoy than in assisting them in developing a personal taste. A more subjective, personal attribute that many people discover to be decisive is a wine's body: some enjoy a light-bodied wine with finesse, while others enjoy only the fullest. Identifying your preferences is one of the most important factors in developing a personal taste, and tasting notes should reflect this emphasis.

Below are listed some of the more popular and readily available types of reds, in order of increasing amounts of body—from lightest to fullest. Following is a list of foods, similarly organized, that often make good matches. Note that these judgments on the relative "weight" of foods are based on simply prepared, relatively unadorned dishes—grilled, for instance. Any substantial sauces, either light or heavy, would make a significant difference in categorizing the food. Furthermore, these categories are the most general of descriptions, and exceptions will abound.

Wine

Light-bodied

—————— Beaujolais Nouveau
Beaujolais
Valpolicella
German wines

Medium-bodied

—————— Spanish wines
Chianti
Barbera
pinot noir
Burgundy
Côtes du Rhône

Full-bodied

—————— Bordeaux
Châteauneuf-du-Pape
Hermitage
merlot
syrah
zinfandel
cabernet sauvignon
Brunello di Montalcino
Barbaresco
Barolo

Food

Light-bodied
————————sturdy fish (salmon, tuna, swordfish)
chicken

Medium-bodied
————————duck and game birds
veal
pork

Full-bodied
————————beef
game
lamb

PRODUCER: _____

NAME: _____ VINTAGE: _____ PRICE: _____

COUNTRY AND REGION: _____

COLOR: _____

AROMA AND BOUQUET: _____
_____
_____
_____

TASTE AND TEXTURE: _____
_____
_____
_____

OVERALL IMPRESSION: _____
_____
_____
_____

DATE: _____ WHERE: _____

SHARED WITH: _____

SERVED WITH: _____
_____
_____

OTHER COMMENTS: _____
_____
_____

PRODUCER: _____

NAME: _____VINTAGE:_____PRICE:_____

COUNTRY AND REGION: _____

COLOR: _____

AROMA AND BOUQUET: _____

_____

_____

_____

TASTE AND TEXTURE: _____

_____

_____

_____

OVERALL IMPRESSION: _____

_____

_____

_____

DATE: _____WHERE: _____

SHARED WITH: _____

SERVED WITH: _____

_____

_____

OTHER COMMENTS: _____

_____

_____

PRODUCER: _____

NAME: _____VINTAGE:_____PRICE:_____

COUNTRY AND REGION:_____

COLOR: _____

AROMA AND BOUQUET: _____
_____
_____
_____

TASTE AND TEXTURE:_____
_____
_____
_____

OVERALL IMPRESSION:_____
_____
_____
_____

DATE:_____WHERE: _____

SHARED WITH: _____

SERVED WITH: _____
_____
_____

OTHER COMMENTS: _____
_____
_____

PRODUCER: _____

NAME: _____VINTAGE:_____PRICE:_____

COUNTRY AND REGION: _____

COLOR: _____

AROMA AND BOUQUET: _____
_____
_____
_____

TASTE AND TEXTURE: _____
_____
_____
_____

OVERALL IMPRESSION: _____
_____
_____
_____

DATE: _____WHERE: _____

SHARED WITH: _____

SERVED WITH: _____
_____
_____

OTHER COMMENTS: _____
_____
_____

PRODUCER: _____

NAME: _____VINTAGE:_____PRICE:_____

COUNTRY AND REGION:_____

COLOR: _____

AROMA AND BOUQUET: _____

_____

_____

_____

TASTE AND TEXTURE:_____

_____

_____

_____

OVERALL IMPRESSION:_____

_____

_____

_____

DATE:_____WHERE: _____

SHARED WITH: _____

SERVED WITH: _____

_____

_____

OTHER COMMENTS: _____

_____

_____

PRODUCER: _____

NAME: _____ VINTAGE: _____ PRICE: _____

COUNTRY AND REGION: _____

COLOR: _____

AROMA AND BOUQUET: _____
_____
_____
_____

TASTE AND TEXTURE: _____
_____
_____
_____

OVERALL IMPRESSION: _____
_____
_____
_____

DATE: _____ WHERE: _____

SHARED WITH: _____

SERVED WITH: _____
_____
_____

OTHER COMMENTS: _____
_____
_____

PRODUCER: _____

NAME: _____VINTAGE:_____PRICE:_____

COUNTRY AND REGION: _____

COLOR: _____

AROMA AND BOUQUET: _____
_____
_____
_____

TASTE AND TEXTURE:_____
_____
_____
_____

OVERALL IMPRESSION:_____
_____
_____
_____

DATE:_____WHERE: _____

SHARED WITH: _____

SERVED WITH: _____
_____
_____

OTHER COMMENTS: _____
_____
_____

PRODUCER: _____

NAME: _____ VINTAGE: _____ PRICE: _____

COUNTRY AND REGION: _____

COLOR: _____

AROMA AND BOUQUET: _____
_____
_____
_____

TASTE AND TEXTURE: _____
_____
_____
_____

OVERALL IMPRESSION: _____
_____
_____
_____

DATE: _____ WHERE: _____

SHARED WITH: _____

SERVED WITH: _____
_____
_____

OTHER COMMENTS: _____
_____
_____

PRODUCER: _____

NAME: _____VINTAGE:_____PRICE:_____

COUNTRY AND REGION:_____

COLOR: _____

AROMA AND BOUQUET: _____

_____

_____

_____

TASTE AND TEXTURE:_____

_____

_____

_____

OVERALL IMPRESSION:_____

_____

_____

_____

DATE:_____WHERE: _____

SHARED WITH: _____

SERVED WITH: _____

_____

_____

OTHER COMMENTS: _____

_____

_____

PRODUCER: _____

NAME: _____ VINTAGE: _____ PRICE: _____

COUNTRY AND REGION: _____

COLOR: _____

AROMA AND BOUQUET: _____
_____
_____
_____

TASTE AND TEXTURE: _____
_____
_____
_____

OVERALL IMPRESSION: _____
_____
_____
_____

DATE: _____ WHERE: _____

SHARED WITH: _____

SERVED WITH: _____
_____
_____

OTHER COMMENTS: _____
_____
_____

PRODUCER: _____

NAME: _____VINTAGE:_____PRICE:_____

COUNTRY AND REGION: _____

COLOR: _____

AROMA AND BOUQUET: _____
_____
_____
_____

TASTE AND TEXTURE: _____
_____
_____
_____

OVERALL IMPRESSION: _____
_____
_____
_____

DATE: _____WHERE: _____

SHARED WITH: _____

SERVED WITH: _____
_____
_____

OTHER COMMENTS: _____
_____
_____

PRODUCER: _____

NAME: _____VINTAGE:_____PRICE:_____

COUNTRY AND REGION: _____

COLOR: _____

AROMA AND BOUQUET: _____

_____

_____

_____

TASTE AND TEXTURE: _____

_____

_____

_____

OVERALL IMPRESSION: _____

_____

_____

_____

DATE: _____WHERE: _____

SHARED WITH: _____

SERVED WITH: _____

_____

_____

OTHER COMMENTS: _____

_____

_____

PRODUCER: _____

NAME: _____VINTAGE:_____PRICE:_____

COUNTRY AND REGION:_____

COLOR: _____

AROMA AND BOUQUET: _____

_____

_____

_____

TASTE AND TEXTURE:_____

_____

_____

_____

OVERALL IMPRESSION:_____

_____

_____

_____

DATE:_____WHERE: _____

SHARED WITH: _____

SERVED WITH: _____

_____

_____

OTHER COMMENTS: _____

_____

_____

PRODUCER: _____

NAME: _____ VINTAGE: _____ PRICE: _____

COUNTRY AND REGION: _____

COLOR: _____

AROMA AND BOUQUET: _____

_____

_____

_____

TASTE AND TEXTURE: _____

_____

_____

_____

OVERALL IMPRESSION: _____

_____

_____

_____

DATE: _____ WHERE: _____

SHARED WITH: _____

SERVED WITH: _____

_____

_____

OTHER COMMENTS: _____

_____

_____

PRODUCER: _____

NAME: _____VINTAGE:_____PRICE:_____

COUNTRY AND REGION:_____

COLOR: _____

AROMA AND BOUQUET: _____
_____
_____
_____

TASTE AND TEXTURE:_____
_____
_____
_____

OVERALL IMPRESSION:_____
_____
_____
_____

DATE:_____WHERE: _____

SHARED WITH: _____

SERVED WITH: _____
_____
_____

OTHER COMMENTS: _____
_____
_____

PRODUCER: _____

NAME: _____ VINTAGE: _____ PRICE: _____

COUNTRY AND REGION: _____

COLOR: _____

AROMA AND BOUQUET: _____
_____
_____
_____

TASTE AND TEXTURE: _____
_____
_____
_____

OVERALL IMPRESSION: _____
_____
_____
_____

DATE: _____ WHERE: _____

SHARED WITH: _____

SERVED WITH: _____
_____
_____

OTHER COMMENTS: _____
_____
_____

PRODUCER: _____

NAME: _____VINTAGE:_____PRICE:_____

COUNTRY AND REGION:_____

COLOR: _____

AROMA AND BOUQUET: _____

_____

_____

_____

TASTE AND TEXTURE:_____

_____

_____

_____

OVERALL IMPRESSION:_____

_____

_____

_____

DATE:_____WHERE: _____

SHARED WITH: _____

SERVED WITH: _____

_____

_____

OTHER COMMENTS: _____

_____

_____

PRODUCER: _____

NAME: _____ VINTAGE: _____ PRICE: _____

COUNTRY AND REGION: _____

COLOR: _____

AROMA AND BOUQUET: _____
_____
_____
_____

TASTE AND TEXTURE: _____
_____
_____
_____

OVERALL IMPRESSION: _____
_____
_____
_____

DATE: _____ WHERE: _____

SHARED WITH: _____

SERVED WITH: _____
_____
_____

OTHER COMMENTS: _____
_____
_____

PRODUCER: _____

NAME: _____ VINTAGE: _____ PRICE: _____

COUNTRY AND REGION: _____

COLOR: _____

AROMA AND BOUQUET: _____

_____

_____

_____

TASTE AND TEXTURE: _____

_____

_____

_____

OVERALL IMPRESSION: _____

_____

_____

_____

DATE: _____ WHERE: _____

SHARED WITH: _____

SERVED WITH: _____

_____

_____

OTHER COMMENTS: _____

_____

_____

PRODUCER: _____

NAME: _____ VINTAGE: _____ PRICE: _____

COUNTRY AND REGION: _____

COLOR: _____

AROMA AND BOUQUET: _____
_____
_____
_____

TASTE AND TEXTURE: _____
_____
_____
_____

OVERALL IMPRESSION: _____
_____
_____
_____

DATE: _____ WHERE: _____

SHARED WITH: _____

SERVED WITH: _____
_____
_____

OTHER COMMENTS: _____
_____
_____

PRODUCER: _____

NAME: _____ VINTAGE: _____ PRICE: _____

COUNTRY AND REGION: _____

COLOR: _____

AROMA AND BOUQUET: _____

_____

_____

_____

TASTE AND TEXTURE: _____

_____

_____

_____

OVERALL IMPRESSION: _____

_____

_____

_____

DATE: _____ WHERE: _____

SHARED WITH: _____

SERVED WITH: _____

_____

_____

OTHER COMMENTS: _____

_____

_____

PRODUCER: _____

NAME: _____ VINTAGE: _____ PRICE: _____

COUNTRY AND REGION: _____

COLOR: _____

AROMA AND BOUQUET: _____
_____
_____
_____

TASTE AND TEXTURE: _____
_____
_____
_____

OVERALL IMPRESSION: _____
_____
_____
_____

DATE: _____ WHERE: _____

SHARED WITH: _____

SERVED WITH: _____
_____
_____

OTHER COMMENTS: _____
_____
_____

PRODUCER: _____

NAME: _____ VINTAGE: _____ PRICE: _____

COUNTRY AND REGION: _____

COLOR: _____

AROMA AND BOUQUET: _____
_____
_____
_____

TASTE AND TEXTURE: _____
_____
_____
_____

DATE: _____ WHERE: _____

OVERALL IMPRESSION: _____
_____
_____
_____

SHARED WITH: _____

SERVED WITH: _____
_____
_____

OTHER COMMENTS: _____
_____
_____

PRODUCER: _____

NAME: _____ VINTAGE: _____ PRICE: _____

COUNTRY AND REGION: _____

COLOR: _____

AROMA AND BOUQUET: _____
_____
_____
_____

TASTE AND TEXTURE: _____
_____
_____
_____

DATE: _____ WHERE: _____

OVERALL IMPRESSION: _____
_____
_____
_____

SHARED WITH: _____

SERVED WITH: _____
_____
_____

OTHER COMMENTS: _____
_____
_____

PRODUCER: _____

NAME: _____ VINTAGE: _____ PRICE: _____

COUNTRY AND REGION: _____

COLOR: _____

AROMA AND BOUQUET: _____
_____
_____
_____

TASTE AND TEXTURE: _____
_____
_____
_____

DATE: _____ WHERE: _____

OVERALL IMPRESSION: _____
_____
_____
_____

SHARED WITH: _____

SERVED WITH: _____
_____
_____

OTHER COMMENTS: _____
_____
_____

PRODUCER: _____

NAME: _____VINTAGE:_____PRICE:_____

COUNTRY AND REGION: _____

COLOR: _____

AROMA AND BOUQUET: _____
_____
_____
_____

TASTE AND TEXTURE: _____
_____
_____
_____

DATE: _____WHERE: _____

OVERALL IMPRESSION: _____
_____
_____
_____

SHARED WITH: _____

SERVED WITH: _____
_____
_____

OTHER COMMENTS: _____
_____
_____

PRODUCER: _____

NAME: _____VINTAGE:_____PRICE:_____

COUNTRY AND REGION: _____

COLOR: _____

AROMA AND BOUQUET:_____
_____
_____
_____

TASTE AND TEXTURE: _____
_____
_____
_____

DATE:_____WHERE: _____

OVERALL IMPRESSION:_____
_____
_____
_____

SHARED WITH: _____

SERVED WITH: _____
_____
_____

OTHER COMMENTS: _____
_____
_____

PRODUCER: _____

NAME: _____VINTAGE:_____PRICE:_____

COUNTRY AND REGION:_____

COLOR: _____

AROMA AND BOUQUET:_____

_____

_____

_____

TASTE AND TEXTURE: _____

_____

_____

_____

DATE:_____WHERE: _____

OVERALL IMPRESSION:_____

_____

_____

_____

SHARED WITH: _____

SERVED WITH: _____

_____

_____

OTHER COMMENTS: _____

_____

_____

PRODUCER: _____

NAME: _____VINTAGE:_____PRICE:_____

COUNTRY AND REGION:_____

COLOR: _____

AROMA AND BOUQUET:_____
_____
_____
_____

TASTE AND TEXTURE: _____
_____
_____
_____

DATE:_____WHERE: _____

OVERALL IMPRESSION:_____
_____
_____
_____

SHARED WITH: _____

SERVED WITH: _____
_____
_____

OTHER COMMENTS: _____
_____
_____

PRODUCER: _____

NAME: _____VINTAGE:_____PRICE:_____

COUNTRY AND REGION: _____

COLOR: _____

AROMA AND BOUQUET: _____
_____
_____
_____

TASTE AND TEXTURE: _____
_____
_____
_____

DATE: _____WHERE: _____

OVERALL IMPRESSION: _____
_____
_____
_____

SHARED WITH: _____

SERVED WITH: _____
_____
_____

OTHER COMMENTS: _____
_____
_____

White Wines

*I*t is often logically but mistakenly assumed that red wines are made exclusively from grapes with red and purple skins, and white wines are made exclusively from grapes with white, yellow, or green skins. In fact, just as decisive as the skin color is the amount of time during fermentation that the *must*—the grape juice—spends in contact with the skins, which contain the coloring pigments: more time produces more color. If the skins are removed from the must almost immediately—within a few hours—the wine will be white, regardless of the grapes' color.

In addition to imparting color to wine, the grapes' solids—skins, stems, and seeds—also include the tannins and oils that imbue a wine with many of its characteristics, including its aging properties. Therefore, as a rule, white wines are less complex, and develop less through aging, than red wines. This is not to say that white wines are inferior to red wines, but they do have different properties.

Perhaps most important among these differences are white wines' vast ranges of flavors and degrees of sweetness. Unlike red wines, some of the most enjoyable whites are the sweeter ones, such as Gewürztraminers, Rieslings, and Sauternes. And light, dry white wines—Chablis, Pouilly-Fuissé, Orvietto—can be satisfying where their light, dry red counterparts would seem thin.

Below are listed some of the more popular and readily available whites, in order of increasing amounts of body—from lightest to fullest. Following is a list of foods, similarly organized, that might make good matches. Note that, just as with the red wines, these judgments on the relative "weight" of foods are based on simply prepared, relatively unadorned dishes. These are general categories, and exceptions will abound.

Wine

Light-bodied

——————— Italian
German
pinot grigio
riesling
Alsace

Medium-bodied

——————— chenin blanc
pinot blanc
sauvignon blanc
Bordeaux
Gewürztraminer
Chablis

Full-bodied

——————— chardonnay
Burgundy
Rhône

Food

Light-bodied

————— delicate, flaky fish (sole, e.g.)
clams and oysters

Medium-bodied

————— sturdy, flaky fish (snapper, e.g.)
shrimp and scallops
lobster

Full-bodied

————— sturdy fish (salmon, tuna, swordfish, e.g.)
veal scallops
chicken cutlets
duck

PRODUCER: _____

NAME: _____VINTAGE:_____PRICE:_____

COUNTRY AND REGION: _____

COLOR: _____

AROMA AND BOUQUET: _____
_____
_____
_____

TASTE AND TEXTURE:_____
_____
_____
_____

OVERALL IMPRESSION:_____
_____
_____
_____

DATE:_____WHERE: _____

SHARED WITH: _____

SERVED WITH: _____
_____
_____

OTHER COMMENTS: _____
_____
_____

PRODUCER: _____

NAME: _____ VINTAGE: _____ PRICE: _____

COUNTRY AND REGION: _____

COLOR: _____

AROMA AND BOUQUET: _____
_____
_____
_____

TASTE AND TEXTURE: _____
_____
_____
_____

OVERALL IMPRESSION: _____
_____
_____
_____

DATE: _____ WHERE: _____

SHARED WITH: _____

SERVED WITH: _____
_____
_____

OTHER COMMENTS: _____
_____
_____

PRODUCER: _____

NAME: _____ VINTAGE: _____ PRICE: _____

COUNTRY AND REGION: _____

COLOR: _____

AROMA AND BOUQUET: _____
_____
_____
_____

TASTE AND TEXTURE: _____
_____
_____
_____

OVERALL IMPRESSION: _____
_____
_____
_____

DATE: _____ WHERE: _____

SHARED WITH: _____

SERVED WITH: _____
_____
_____

OTHER COMMENTS: _____
_____
_____

PRODUCER: _____

NAME: _____ VINTAGE: _____ PRICE: _____

COUNTRY AND REGION: _____

COLOR: _____

AROMA AND BOUQUET: _____
_____
_____
_____

TASTE AND TEXTURE: _____
_____
_____
_____

OVERALL IMPRESSION: _____
_____
_____
_____

DATE: _____ WHERE: _____

SHARED WITH: _____

SERVED WITH: _____
_____
_____

OTHER COMMENTS: _____
_____
_____

PRODUCER: _____

NAME: _____VINTAGE:_____PRICE:_____

COUNTRY AND REGION: _____

COLOR: _____

AROMA AND BOUQUET: _____
_____
_____
_____

TASTE AND TEXTURE: _____
_____
_____
_____

OVERALL IMPRESSION: _____
_____
_____
_____

DATE: _____WHERE: _____

SHARED WITH: _____

SERVED WITH: _____
_____
_____

OTHER COMMENTS: _____
_____
_____

PRODUCER: _____

NAME: _____ VINTAGE: _____ PRICE: _____

COUNTRY AND REGION: _____

COLOR: _____

AROMA AND BOUQUET: _____
_____
_____
_____

TASTE AND TEXTURE: _____
_____
_____
_____

OVERALL IMPRESSION: _____
_____
_____
_____

DATE: _____ WHERE: _____

SHARED WITH: _____

SERVED WITH: _____
_____
_____

OTHER COMMENTS: _____
_____
_____

PRODUCER: _____

NAME: _____ VINTAGE: _____ PRICE: _____

COUNTRY AND REGION: _____

COLOR: _____

AROMA AND BOUQUET: _____
_____
_____
_____

TASTE AND TEXTURE: _____
_____
_____
_____

OVERALL IMPRESSION: _____
_____
_____
_____

DATE: _____ WHERE: _____

SHARED WITH: _____

SERVED WITH: _____
_____
_____

OTHER COMMENTS: _____
_____
_____

PRODUCER: _____

NAME: _____VINTAGE:_____PRICE:_____

COUNTRY AND REGION:_____

COLOR: _____

AROMA AND BOUQUET: _____
_____
_____
_____

TASTE AND TEXTURE:_____
_____
_____
_____

OVERALL IMPRESSION:_____
_____
_____
_____

DATE:_____WHERE: _____

SHARED WITH: _____

SERVED WITH: _____
_____
_____

OTHER COMMENTS: _____
_____
_____

PRODUCER: _____

NAME: _____VINTAGE:_____PRICE:_____

COUNTRY AND REGION:_____

COLOR: _____

AROMA AND BOUQUET: _____
_____
_____
_____

TASTE AND TEXTURE:_____
_____
_____
_____

OVERALL IMPRESSION:_____
_____
_____
_____

DATE: _____WHERE: _____

SHARED WITH: _____

SERVED WITH: _____
_____
_____

OTHER COMMENTS: _____
_____
_____

PRODUCER: _____

NAME: _____ VINTAGE: _____ PRICE: _____

COUNTRY AND REGION: _____

COLOR: _____

AROMA AND BOUQUET: _____
_____
_____
_____

TASTE AND TEXTURE: _____
_____
_____
_____

OVERALL IMPRESSION: _____
_____
_____
_____

DATE: _____ WHERE: _____

SHARED WITH: _____

SERVED WITH: _____
_____
_____

OTHER COMMENTS: _____
_____
_____

PRODUCER: _____

NAME: _____ VINTAGE: _____ PRICE: _____

COUNTRY AND REGION: _____

COLOR: _____

AROMA AND BOUQUET: _____
_____
_____
_____

TASTE AND TEXTURE: _____
_____
_____
_____

OVERALL IMPRESSION: _____
_____
_____
_____

DATE: _____ WHERE: _____

SHARED WITH: _____

SERVED WITH: _____
_____
_____

OTHER COMMENTS: _____
_____
_____

PRODUCER: _____

NAME: _____VINTAGE:_____PRICE:_____

COUNTRY AND REGION:_____

COLOR: _____

AROMA AND BOUQUET: _____
_____
_____
_____

TASTE AND TEXTURE:_____
_____
_____
_____

OVERALL IMPRESSION:_____
_____
_____
_____

DATE:_____WHERE: _____

SHARED WITH: _____

SERVED WITH: _____
_____
_____

OTHER COMMENTS: _____
_____
_____

PRODUCER: _____

NAME: _____ VINTAGE:_____ PRICE:_____

COUNTRY AND REGION:_____

COLOR: _____

AROMA AND BOUQUET: _____
_____
_____
_____

TASTE AND TEXTURE:_____
_____
_____
_____
_____

OVERALL IMPRESSION:_____
_____
_____
_____

DATE:_____ WHERE: _____

SHARED WITH: _____

SERVED WITH: _____
_____
_____

OTHER COMMENTS: _____
_____
_____

PRODUCER: _____

NAME: _____VINTAGE: _____PRICE: _____

COUNTRY AND REGION: _____

COLOR: _____

AROMA AND BOUQUET: _____
_____
_____
_____

TASTE AND TEXTURE: _____
_____
_____
_____

OVERALL IMPRESSION: _____
_____
_____
_____

DATE: _____WHERE: _____

SHARED WITH: _____

SERVED WITH: _____
_____
_____

OTHER COMMENTS: _____
_____
_____

PRODUCER: _____

NAME: _____ VINTAGE: _____ PRICE: _____

COUNTRY AND REGION: _____

COLOR: _____

AROMA AND BOUQUET: _____
_____
_____
_____

TASTE AND TEXTURE: _____
_____
_____
_____

OVERALL IMPRESSION: _____
_____
_____
_____

DATE: _____ WHERE: _____

SHARED WITH: _____

SERVED WITH: _____
_____
_____

OTHER COMMENTS: _____
_____
_____

PRODUCER: _____

NAME: _____ VINTAGE: _____ PRICE: _____

COUNTRY AND REGION: _____

COLOR: _____

AROMA AND BOUQUET: _____
_____
_____
_____

TASTE AND TEXTURE: _____
_____
_____
_____

OVERALL IMPRESSION: _____
_____
_____
_____

DATE: _____ WHERE: _____

SHARED WITH: _____

SERVED WITH: _____
_____
_____

OTHER COMMENTS: _____
_____
_____

PRODUCER: _____

NAME: _____VINTAGE:_____PRICE:_____

COUNTRY AND REGION:_____

COLOR: _____

AROMA AND BOUQUET: _____
_____
_____
_____

TASTE AND TEXTURE:_____
_____
_____
_____

OVERALL IMPRESSION:_____
_____
_____
_____

DATE:_____WHERE: _____

SHARED WITH: _____

SERVED WITH: _____
_____
_____

OTHER COMMENTS: _____
_____
_____

PRODUCER: _____

NAME: _____ VINTAGE: _____ PRICE: _____

COUNTRY AND REGION: _____

COLOR: _____

AROMA AND BOUQUET: _____
_____
_____
_____

TASTE AND TEXTURE: _____
_____
_____
_____

OVERALL IMPRESSION: _____
_____
_____
_____

DATE: _____ WHERE: _____

SHARED WITH: _____

SERVED WITH: _____
_____
_____

OTHER COMMENTS: _____
_____
_____

PRODUCER: _____

NAME: _____VINTAGE:_____PRICE:_____

COUNTRY AND REGION:_____

COLOR: _____

AROMA AND BOUQUET: _____
_____
_____
_____

TASTE AND TEXTURE:_____
_____
_____
_____

OVERALL IMPRESSION:_____
_____
_____
_____

DATE:_____WHERE: _____

SHARED WITH: _____

SERVED WITH: _____
_____
_____

OTHER COMMENTS: _____
_____
_____

PRODUCER: _____

NAME: _____VINTAGE:_____PRICE:_____

COUNTRY AND REGION:_____

COLOR: _____

AROMA AND BOUQUET: _____

_____

_____

_____

TASTE AND TEXTURE:_____

_____

_____

_____

OVERALL IMPRESSION:_____

_____

_____

_____

DATE:_____WHERE: _____

SHARED WITH: _____

SERVED WITH: _____

_____

_____

OTHER COMMENTS: _____

_____

_____

PRODUCER: _____

NAME: _____ VINTAGE: _____ PRICE: _____

COUNTRY AND REGION: _____

COLOR: _____

AROMA AND BOUQUET: _____
_____
_____
_____

TASTE AND TEXTURE: _____
_____
_____
_____

OVERALL IMPRESSION: _____
_____
_____
_____

DATE: _____ WHERE: _____

SHARED WITH: _____

SERVED WITH: _____
_____
_____

OTHER COMMENTS: _____
_____
_____

PRODUCER: _____

NAME: _____VINTAGE:_____PRICE:_____

COUNTRY AND REGION: _____

COLOR: _____

AROMA AND BOUQUET: _____

_____

_____

_____

TASTE AND TEXTURE: _____

_____

_____

_____

OVERALL IMPRESSION: _____

_____

_____

_____

DATE: _____WHERE: _____

SHARED WITH: _____

SERVED WITH: _____

_____

_____

OTHER COMMENTS: _____

_____

_____

PRODUCER: _____

NAME: _____VINTAGE:_____PRICE:_____

COUNTRY AND REGION:_____

COLOR: _____

AROMA AND BOUQUET: _____
_____
_____
_____

TASTE AND TEXTURE:_____
_____
_____
_____

OVERALL IMPRESSION:_____
_____
_____
_____

DATE:_____WHERE: _____

SHARED WITH: _____

SERVED WITH: _____
_____
_____

OTHER COMMENTS: _____
_____
_____

PRODUCER: _____

NAME: _____ VINTAGE: _____ PRICE: _____

COUNTRY AND REGION: _____

COLOR: _____

AROMA AND BOUQUET: _____
_____
_____
_____

TASTE AND TEXTURE: _____
_____
_____
_____
_____

DATE: _____ WHERE: _____

OVERALL IMPRESSION: _____
_____
_____
_____

SHARED WITH: _____

SERVED WITH: _____
_____
_____

OTHER COMMENTS: _____
_____
_____

PRODUCER: _____

NAME: _____ VINTAGE: _____ PRICE: _____

COUNTRY AND REGION: _____

COLOR: _____

AROMA AND BOUQUET: _____
_____
_____
_____

TASTE AND TEXTURE: _____
_____
_____
_____

DATE: _____ WHERE: _____

OVERALL IMPRESSION: _____
_____
_____
_____

SHARED WITH: _____

SERVED WITH: _____
_____
_____

OTHER COMMENTS: _____
_____
_____

PRODUCER: _____

NAME: _____VINTAGE: _____PRICE: _____

COUNTRY AND REGION: _____

COLOR: _____

AROMA AND BOUQUET: _____
_____
_____
_____

TASTE AND TEXTURE: _____
_____
_____
_____

DATE: _____WHERE: _____

OVERALL IMPRESSION: _____
_____
_____
_____

SHARED WITH: _____

SERVED WITH: _____
_____
_____

OTHER COMMENTS: _____
_____
_____

PRODUCER: _____

NAME: _____VINTAGE:_____PRICE:_____

COUNTRY AND REGION:_____

COLOR: _____

AROMA AND BOUQUET:_____
_____
_____
_____

TASTE AND TEXTURE: _____
_____
_____
_____

DATE:_____WHERE: _____

OVERALL IMPRESSION:_____
_____
_____
_____

SHARED WITH: _____

SERVED WITH: _____
_____
_____

OTHER COMMENTS: _____
_____
_____

PRODUCER: _____

NAME: _____ VINTAGE: _____ PRICE: _____

COUNTRY AND REGION: _____

COLOR: _____

AROMA AND BOUQUET: _____
_____
_____
_____

TASTE AND TEXTURE: _____
_____
_____
_____

DATE: _____ WHERE: _____

OVERALL IMPRESSION: _____
_____
_____
_____

SHARED WITH: _____

SERVED WITH: _____
_____
_____

OTHER COMMENTS: _____
_____
_____

PRODUCER: _____

NAME: _____VINTAGE:_____PRICE:_____

COUNTRY AND REGION: _____

COLOR: _____

AROMA AND BOUQUET: _____
_____
_____
_____

TASTE AND TEXTURE: _____
_____
_____
_____

DATE: _____WHERE: _____

OVERALL IMPRESSION: _____
_____
_____
_____

SHARED WITH: _____

SERVED WITH: _____
_____
_____

OTHER COMMENTS: _____
_____
_____

PRODUCER: _____

NAME: _____VINTAGE:_____PRICE:_____

COUNTRY AND REGION: _____

COLOR: _____

AROMA AND BOUQUET: _____
_____
_____
_____

TASTE AND TEXTURE: _____
_____
_____
_____

DATE: _____WHERE: _____

OVERALL IMPRESSION: _____
_____
_____
_____

SHARED WITH: _____

SERVED WITH: _____
_____
_____

OTHER COMMENTS: _____
_____
_____

Sparkling Wines

S nobbiness aside, there is an excellent reason to distinguish between Champagne and all other sparkling, or effervescent, wines: only about 2 percent of the worldwide production of sparkling wine is actually from the Champagne region of France's Marne Valley. But this region produces exceptional—and exceptionally well known—sparkling wines, including Perrier-Jouët, Louis Roederer, Veuve Clicquot-Ponsardin, Moët et Chandon (the largest), Bollinger, Krug, Mumm, Piper Heidsieck, and Taittinger, among others.

Furthermore, many of these *grandes marques* ("great brands") also produce *cuvée de prestige* or *cuvée spéciale* premium vintage wines, made only in the best years, which account for fewer than 5 percent of bona fide Champagnes: these include Belle Epoque (from Perrier-Jouët), Cristal (Roederer), and La Grande Dame (Veuve Clicquot-Ponsardin). Perhaps the most widely known of these premium Champagnes is Dom Pérignon (Moët et Chandon), named after a seventeenth-century cellarmaster of the Abbey of Hautvillers who, contrary to popular belief, didn't invent Champagne, but is credited with refining the *méthode champenoise* production process.

Given the tiny percentage of sparkling wine that's actually Champagne, and given the tiny percentage of Champagne that's premium or vintage, it stands to reason that these wines are not only quite expensive (usually at least seventy-five dollars per bottle) but also hard to find. And it also stands to reason that there are many, *many* excellent non-Champagne sparkling wines produced throughout the winemaking world.

One of the most important traits to note on the label of a sparkling wine is the extent to which it is dry, or *sec:* in order of decreasing dryness (increasing sweetness, caused by residual sugar) the terms are *brut, extra-sec, sec, demi-sec,* and *doux* (sweet). Your preference for sweetness will greatly influence which wine you will enjoy most—if you're inclined toward the dry and despise the sweet, you will usually be better off with an inexpensive brut than with the most prestigious demi-sec.

Also on the label will be the vintage year, if any—and don't be surprised or taken aback if there is no year. Most sparkling wines, including Champagnes, are *nonvintage*—are not produced from the required high percentage (usually about 80 percent, depending on the governing body) of grapes from a single year, but are *cuvées,* or blends, of grapes from different years. The exact proportions of these blends are among the most closely guarded wine secrets in the world. The presence or absence of a vintage year usually has almost nothing to do with the quality of the wine.

A final word: Americans tend to drink sparkling wine only on celebratory occasions—New Year's Eve, weddings, and so forth. This may be because we too closely associate sparkling wine with premium Champagne—and with this association comes a forbidding price tag. But the vast majority of sparkling wines are no more expensive than other wines, and can be enjoyed in a wide variety of situations.

PRODUCER: _____

NAME: _____ VINTAGE: _____ PRICE: _____

COUNTRY AND REGION: _____

COLOR: _____

AROMA AND BOUQUET: _____
_____
_____
_____

TASTE AND TEXTURE: _____
_____
_____
_____

OVERALL IMPRESSION: _____
_____
_____
_____

DATE: _____ WHERE: _____

SHARED WITH: _____

SERVED WITH: _____
_____
_____

OTHER COMMENTS: _____
_____
_____

PRODUCER: _____

NAME: _____VINTAGE:_____PRICE:_____

COUNTRY AND REGION:_____

COLOR: _____

AROMA AND BOUQUET: _____
_____
_____
_____

TASTE AND TEXTURE:_____
_____
_____
_____

OVERALL IMPRESSION:_____
_____
_____
_____

DATE:_____WHERE: _____

SHARED WITH: _____

SERVED WITH: _____
_____
_____

OTHER COMMENTS: _____
_____
_____

PRODUCER: _____

NAME: _____ VINTAGE: _____ PRICE: _____

COUNTRY AND REGION: _____

COLOR: _____

AROMA AND BOUQUET: _____
_____
_____
_____

TASTE AND TEXTURE: _____
_____
_____
_____

OVERALL IMPRESSION: _____
_____
_____
_____

DATE: _____ WHERE: _____

SHARED WITH: _____

SERVED WITH: _____
_____
_____

OTHER COMMENTS: _____
_____
_____

PRODUCER: _____

NAME: _____VINTAGE:_____PRICE:_____

COUNTRY AND REGION:_____

COLOR: _____

AROMA AND BOUQUET: _____

_____

_____

_____

TASTE AND TEXTURE:_____

_____

_____

_____

OVERALL IMPRESSION:_____

_____

_____

_____

DATE:_____WHERE: _____

SHARED WITH: _____

SERVED WITH: _____

_____

_____

OTHER COMMENTS: _____

_____

_____

PRODUCER: _____

NAME: _____ VINTAGE: ____ PRICE: ____

COUNTRY AND REGION: _____

COLOR: _____

AROMA AND BOUQUET: _____
_____
_____
_____

TASTE AND TEXTURE: _____
_____
_____
_____

OVERALL IMPRESSION: _____
_____
_____
_____

DATE: _____ WHERE: _____

SHARED WITH: _____

SERVED WITH: _____
_____
_____

OTHER COMMENTS: _____
_____
_____

PRODUCER: _____

NAME: _____ VINTAGE: _____ PRICE: _____

COUNTRY AND REGION: _____

COLOR: _____

AROMA AND BOUQUET: _____

_____

_____

_____

TASTE AND TEXTURE: _____

_____

_____

_____

OVERALL IMPRESSION: _____

_____

_____

_____

DATE: _____ WHERE: _____

SHARED WITH: _____

SERVED WITH: _____

_____

_____

OTHER COMMENTS: _____

_____

_____

PRODUCER: _____

NAME: _____VINTAGE:_____PRICE:_____

COUNTRY AND REGION:_____

COLOR: _____

AROMA AND BOUQUET: _____
_____
_____
_____

TASTE AND TEXTURE:_____
_____
_____
_____

OVERALL IMPRESSION:_____
_____
_____
_____

DATE:_____WHERE: _____

SHARED WITH: _____

SERVED WITH: _____
_____
_____

OTHER COMMENTS: _____
_____
_____

PRODUCER: _____

NAME: _____ VINTAGE: _____ PRICE: _____

COUNTRY AND REGION: _____

COLOR: _____

AROMA AND BOUQUET: _____
_____
_____
_____

TASTE AND TEXTURE: _____
_____
_____
_____

OVERALL IMPRESSION: _____
_____
_____
_____

DATE: _____ WHERE: _____

SHARED WITH: _____

SERVED WITH: _____
_____
_____

OTHER COMMENTS: _____
_____
_____

PRODUCER: _____

NAME: _____ VINTAGE: _____ PRICE: _____

COUNTRY AND REGION: _____

COLOR: _____

AROMA AND BOUQUET: _____

_____

_____

_____

TASTE AND TEXTURE: _____

_____

_____

_____

_____

OVERALL IMPRESSION: _____

_____

_____

_____

DATE: _____ WHERE: _____

SHARED WITH: _____

SERVED WITH: _____

_____

_____

OTHER COMMENTS: _____

_____

_____

Glossary

*T*he vocabulary of wine is a language unto itself, including technical terms from agriculture, production, geography, and tasting, with many words and names from a few different languages thrown in for good, confusing measure. Furthermore, the meanings of some terms have changed over the years; some terms have multiple meanings that are completely unrelated to one another; some terms don't have any commonly agreed-upon meanings whatsoever, and therefore mean practically nothing; and some terms (particularly French) have meanings so complex, often based on obscure history, that grasping their import is beyond the ken of anyone other than the most dedicated enophile.

The pages that follow do not cover this entire language. Rather, this is a list of commonly encountered terms that will assist you in making tasting notes, especially toward the end of reading the label and understanding its components, so you can accurately note the defining aspects of the wine. These encompass geographic and varietal terms, which are, in addition to the makers and vintages, the primary definitions of wines; some general tasting-related concepts; and a number of commonly encountered foreign words. Tasting adjectives are omitted because of the impossibility of meaningfully defining them with text alone (actual *tasting* is required to define them); specific wine names are omitted because of their near infinite number; agricultural and production terms are omitted because nothing short of a complete education on the subject will meaningfully assist in tasting and remembering wines.

acidity: Important and natural taste characteristic, objectionable only when out of balance with other elements.

aftertaste: Lingering impression on the palate after the wine has been swallowed, outlasting other sensations.

Alsace: German-influenced region in northeast France, peculiar in that many of its wines are labeled as varietals rather than for the region or subregion, the more common practice in France.

American Viticultural Area (AVA): A designated geographic growing area, the United States' parallel to the French or other international *appellations,* but AVAs do not impose strict wine-production regulations.

appellation: Designated geographical growing area whose wines' production, grapes, labeling, and other aspects fall under the supervision and standardization of a governing body.

Appellation d'Origine Contrôlée (AOC or AC): France's governing body for designated growing areas.

Armagnac: French region and eponymous fine brandy, aged in local black oak.

aroma: Fruity fragrance of the grape variety, usually associated with young wines; distinguished from bouquet, the more complex fragrance that develops during aging.

***Asti* (or *Asti Spumante*):** Region within Italy's Piedmont and eponymous well-known Italian sparkling wine produced from muscat grapes.

balance: Wine's quality of having a harmonious combination of all taste characteristics, with none overwhelming.

Barbaresco: Region within Italy's Piedmont known for rich, dry reds made from nebbiolo grapes.

Barolo: Region within Italy's Piedmont known for rich, full-bodied reds made from nebbiolo grapes, often considered the best Italian wines.

Beaujolais: Region within France's Burgundy known for light, fruity reds.

Beaujolais Nouveau: Category of young red wine from the eponymous region of France's Burgundy, released annually—and strictly—on the third Thursday of November.

bianco: Italian, "white."

blanc de blancs: Usually a Champagne made from white-wine pinot noir grapes only, rather than from a mixture of white- and red-wine grapes; but sometimes used to refer to other white wines, still or sparkling, made from white-wine grapes only.

blending: Creating a single superior wine by combining different lesser ones.

blush: Often sweet wine made from red-wine grapes.

body: Quality of wine's consistency—sometimes referred to as weight, or texture—as a sensation in the mouth, ranging from thin (or light) to full.

Bordeaux: Region in southwest France, probably the most well-known and respected. Encompasses the districts Graves, Médoc (includes the communes Margaux, Pauillac, Saint-Estèphe, and Saint-Julien), Pomerol, Saint-Émilion, and Sauternes, with over fifty individual appellations and thousands of châteaux, including the famed Haut-Brion, Lafite-Rothschild, Latour, and Margaux (the only four to have received a *premier cru* ranking in the Classification of 1855). Wines are usually blends of different grapes, rather than varietals, primarily cabernet sauvignon, cabernet franc, and merlot for medium- to full-bodied reds, and sauvignon blanc, sémillon, and muscadelle for full-bodied whites.

bouquet: Fully complex fragrance of mature wine.

brandy: Wood-aged liquor distilled from wine.

breathe: Aeration process that occurs when wine is un-corked and exposed to outside air; accelerated by decanting.

brut: Describes the driest sparkling wines, even drier than extra-dry.

Burgundy (or Borgogne): Very well-known region in eastern France, encompassing Beaujolais, Chablis, Côte Chalonnaise, Côte d'Or, and Macônnais, using predominantly pinot noir and gamay for light- to medium-bodied reds, and chardonnay for full-bodied whites.

cabernet franc: Red-wine grape, usually blended, especially with merlot and cabernet sauvignon.

cabernet sauvignon: The most popular and widely used red-wine grape, and the predominant one in Bordeaux and Napa reds; produces dry, full-bodied, and complex wines.

Chablis: District within France's Burgundy, best known for producing dry, light-bodied whites from chardonnay.

Champagne: Region within France's Marne Valley and eponymous sparkling wine, produced according to very strict specifications, usually from chardonnay and pinot noir. Colloquially, used as a generic name for sparkling wines.

chardonnay: The most extensively used white-wine grape, usually produces rich, oaky medium- to full-bodied wines.

château: French, "wine estate"; vineyard; the usual designation in Bordeaux.

Châteauneuf-du-Pape: Region within France's Rhône known for rich, spicy, full-bodied reds.

Chianti: Region in Italy's Tuscany and eponymous dry, light-bodied reds, traditionally available in straw-covered bottles called *fiaschi*. Encompasses seven subzones, the most well-known of which is Chianti Classico.

claret: British term for red Bordeaux wines.

Classification of 1855: Ranking of Bordeaux wines for the Paris Exhibition, dividing châteaux among numbered *crus classés* ("classed growths").

Cognac: Town in western France and eponymous brandy, considered by many to be the finest, often labeled V.S. (very superior), V.S.O.P. (very superior old pale), and V.V.S.O.P. (very, very superior old pale), and sometimes with X.O, Extra, Reserve, or Fine Champagne.

Columbia Valley: Viticultural area in southern Washington State and northern Oregon.

complex: Refers to a wine with a variety of well-balanced bouquet and taste elements.

corked: Wine that is tainted by the disagreeable smell and taste of a mold that develops on faulty corks, estimated to affect as many as 5 percent of all bottles.

cortese: White-wine grape grown in northern Italy, particularly Piedmont and Lombardy, that produces delicate, fruity wines.

Côte Chalonnaise: Region within France's Burgundy known for reds from pinot noir, whites from chardonnay, and the Crémant de Borgogne sparkling wines.

Côte d'Or: Small but famous region within France's Burgundy, near Dijon, divided into Côte de Nuits in the north, known for reds from pinot noir, and Côte de Beaune in the south, known for whites from chardonnay.

Côtes du Rhône: Appellation within France's Rhône, known for medium- to full-bodied reds.

cru: French, "growth," used with an adjective (*premier* or *grand*, for example) to describe a vineyard's ranking.

cuvée: French, "contents of the vat," refers to the blend of a wine, particularly for Champagnes.

demi-sec: French, "half-dry," originally used to describe Champagne drier than most, but now used for sparkling wines sweeter than most.

Denominação de Origem Controlada (DOC): The designation for Portugal's highest-quality wines.

Denominación de Origen (DO) and *Denominación de Origen Calificada (DOCa):* Spain's quality designations, the latter more *calificada* ("qualified").

Denominazione di Origine Controllata (DOC): Italy's governing body for designated growing areas.

Denominazione di Origine Controllata e Garantita (DOCG): A more stringent subdivision of Italy's DOC system, incorporating the Italian government's approval and guarantee of the highest quality.

dolcetto: Red-wine grape from Italy's Piedmont that produces rich, fruity, but dry medium-bodied reds, the most well known of which is Dolcetto d'Alba.

domaine: French, "wine estate," often used in Burgundy.

dry: Taste characteristic of having a very small or no taste of sugar.

fattoria: Italian, "wine estate."

fermentation: Chemical process through which sugar is converted into alcohol—grape juice into wine.

Finger Lakes: American Viticultural Area in central New York State, directly south of Lake Ontario, that produces a substantial portion of non-Californian American wine.

finish: The final sensation of a wine.

fortified: Wine whose natural alcohol level from fermentation is augmented by the addition of a distilled spirit, resulting in an alcohol level of usually 18–19 percent, as opposed to 11–13 percent for table wines. The most widely known are Madeira, Marsala, port, and sherry.

Frascati: Region near Rome known for dry whites.

fruity: Rich fruit flavor, most often of grapes, but also of apples, berries, or others.

fumé blanc (or sauvignon blanc): White-wine grape that produces crisp, dry, herby light- to medium-bodied wines.

gamay: Red-wine grape, the predominant grape of Beaujolais, that accounts for the region's light, fruity wines.

Gattinara: Region within Italy's Piedmont known for full-bodied reds made from nebbiolo grapes.

Gavi: Region within Italy's Piedmont known for high-quality dry whites from cortese grapes.

Gewürztraminer: White-wine grape, popular in France's Alsace, that produces dry, spicy wines.

grand cru: French, "great growth"; the top Burgundy, Champagne, and Alsace vineyard rankings, but not particularly meaningful in Bordeaux.

Graves: Region within France's Bordeaux, unusual in that it is known for crisp, dry whites as well as reds, and includes the only non-Médoc château, Haut-Brion, to have received a *premier cru* ranking in the Classification of 1855.

Gutsabfüllung (or Erzeugerabfüllung): German, "estate bottled."

Hermitage (or Ermitage): Appellation within France's Rhône known for big, full-bodied reds made from syrah as well as very full-bodied whites.

Hunter Valley: Region in New South Wales, Australia.

imbottigliato all'origine: Italian, "estate bottled."

Languedoc-Roussillon: Region in southern France, also called the Midi, known for producing vast quantities of ordinary reds.

Mâconnais: Region within France's Burgundy known for whites made from chardonnay and reds from gamay, and encompasses a number of well-known appellations, including Mâcon-Villages, Pouilly Fuissé, and Saint-Véran.

Madeira: Portuguese island and eponymous fortified wine.

magnum: Bottle that holds 1.5 liters, twice the size of a standard bottle.

Margaux: Appellation within the Médoc region of France's Bordeaux, long considered one of if not the most prestigious producer of red wines made from a blend of grapes.

Marsala: Region in Sicily and eponymous fortified wine.

Médoc: Largest and most famous region within France's Bordeaux, includes the Bas-Médoc and the Haute-Médoc, in which are located all but one (Haut-Brion, in Graves) of the sixty-one châteaux that were rated in the Classification of 1855.

merlot: Red-wine grape, grown worldwide, that produces rich, fruity, full-bodied wines.

mis en bouteille au domaine or *mis en bouteille du château:* French, "estate bottled."

muscadelle: Strongly flavored white-wine grape.

muscat: Grape family with hundreds of varieties, including some used in winemaking.

Napa Valley: America's most famous winemaking region, in Northern California, particularly known for cabernet sauvignon, chardonnay, merlot, and pinot noir varietals.

nebbiolo: Red-wine grape responsible for many of Italy's highest quality full-bodied wines.

N.V.: Nonvintage, or a wine made from grapes harvested in more than a single year, a common practice for sparkling wines, including Champagne.

Orvieto: Region within Italy's Umbria known for ordinary dry whites.

Pauillac: Appellation within the Haut-Médoc region of France's Bordeaux known for full-bodied reds made from cabernet sauvignon, and contains three of the five *premier cru* Bordeaux châteaux, Lafite-Rothschild, Latour, and Mouton-Rothschild.

Piedmont: Region in northern Italy known for reds; includes Barbaresco, Barolo, and Gattinara.

pinot blanc: White-wine grape that produces dry, fresh wines in Alsace, California, and northern Italy.

pinot gris (**French**), *pinot grigio* (**Italian**): White-wine grape that produces widely varying wines, most notably in northern Italy and Alsace.

pinot noir: Red-wine grape, the predominant one in Burgundy, produces fruity, complex wines.

Pomerol: Small district within France's Bordeaux, known for reds made from merlot, and includes the famous Château Pétrus.

port: Sweet, fortified dessert wine from Portugal's Douro Valley, categorized as vintage (the most expensive, sometimes aged fifty or more years), ruby (least expensive, generally aged two years), tawny (blends of different vintages, usually aged ten, twenty, thirty, or forty years), and white.

Pouilly-Fuissé: Region within Burgundy's Mâconnais known for whites made from chardonnay.

Pouilly-Fumé: Region within France's Loire known for medium-bodied whites made from sauvignon blanc.

premier cru: French, "first growth," used in the Classification of 1855 to define four Bordeaux châteaux—Haut-Brion, Lafite-Rothschild, Latour, and Margaux—as producing the best reds in France (a fifth, Mouton-Rothschild, was upgraded in 1973), and eleven Sauternes châteaux as producing the best whites, most famously Châteaux d'Yquem, which was given the additional distinction of *premier grand cru.*

quinta: Portuguese, "farm"; wine estate.

Rhône: River that begins in the Swiss Alps and runs through much of eastern France, whose valley is home to many great wine regions, including Châteauneuf-du-Pape, Côtes du Rhône, Côte Rôtie, Gigondas, Hermitage, and Tavel.

riesling: Important white-wine grape, particularly in Germany, often fruity but complex, ranging from dry to sweet, usually light-bodied.

Rioja: Region in northern Spain known for light- to medium-bodied reds.

rosé (or blanc de noir): Often sweet wine made from red-wine grapes.

rosso: Italian, "red."

Russian River Valley: viticultural area in northern California known primarily for whites.

Saint-Émilion: Region within France's Bordeaux known for reds made from merlot.

Saint-Estèphe: Appellation within the Médoc region of France's Bordeaux known for full-bodied reds.

Saint-Julien: Appellation within the Médoc region of France's Bordeaux known for superb reds made from cabernet sauvignon.

sake: Japanese rice wine.

Sauternes: Appellation within the Graves district of France's Bordeaux and eponymous rich, sweet white wine, made primarily with sémillon grapes.

sauvignon blanc **(or** *fumé blanc):* White-wine grape that produces crisp, dry, herby, light- to medium-bodied wines.

Schloss: German, "castle"; wine estate.

sec **(French),** *secco* **(Italian)***:* Dry when describing still wines, but sweeter than normal when describing sparkling wines.

Sekt: Top category of German sparkling wine.

sémillon: White-wine grape that produces light and crisp but ordinary wines, but very useful in blending with sauvignon blanc.

sherry: Fortified Spanish dessert or aperitif wine, ranges from dry to sweet. Either oloroso, which are aged, dark, rich, and usually served at room temperature; or fino, which are pale, dry, not aged, meant to be drunk young, and usually served chilled.

Soave: Region within Italy's Veneto known for ordinary dry whites.

sommelier: Restaurant's wine steward.

Sonoma County: Region in Northern California, west of the Napa Valley, that produces well-respected reds and whites from a variety of grapes.

sulfites: Salts of sulfurous acid, which is frequently used in viticulture and production (as an insecticide, to prevent mold, etc.), to which some people are extremely allergic.

syrah (or shiraz): Red-wine grape widely planted in Australia, the Rhône, and California; produces rich, spicy, smoky wines.

table wine: No universal definition other than not fortified or sparkling.

tannins: Substances derived mostly from grape skins, seeds, and stems, but also from other factors, including the wood in which wine is aged, that produce astringency and contribute to structure, body, texture, and beneficial aging.

texture: A heavy sensation in the mouth with wines that are full-bodied and intense.

trebbiano: White-wine grape not known for aroma or flavor, but important in blending.

Umpqua Valley: viticultural area in western Oregon.

Valpolicella: Region within Italy's Veneto known for fruity, light-bodied reds.

varietal: A wine named for its primary variety of grape, rather than a region, and the dominant practice in North and South America, Australia, New Zealand, some other New

World areas, and a few distinct regions in Europe. Must be made from a certain percentage (usually 75 percent or more), specified by law, of the grape for which it is named.

vermouth: Fortified, aromatic (flavored with herbs and spices) white wine, either dry, which is used in cocktails or as an aperitif, or sweet, used in sweet cocktails.

vin: French, "wine."

vineyard: Agricultural area in which grapes are grown.

vino: Italian and Spanish, "wine."

vintage: Specifically, the year of a grape harvest, but usually also refers to the year in which the wine was made.

Weingut: German, "wine estate."

Willamette Valley: viticultural area in northern Oregon.

winery: Where wine is made.

zinfandel: Red-wine grape that produces a wide variety of wines (red, white, and sparkling), primarily in California.